Honey In Your Heart

Ways to See and Savor the Simple good Things

Mary anne radmacher

Honey In Your Heart

Ways to See and Savor the Simple good Things

mary anne radmacher

Conari Press

First published in 2012 by Conari Press,
an imprint of Red Wheel/Weiser, LLC

With offices at:

665 Third Street, Suite 400
San Francisco, CA 94107
www.redwheelweiser.com

ISBN: 978-1-57324-479-4

Library of Congress Cataloging-in-Publication Data
available upon request

Cover design by Jim Warner
Text design by Liz Kalloch
Art by Mary Anne Radmacher
Typeset in Democratica, Century Gothic and ITC Novarese.

Printed in Hong Kong
GW

10 9 8 7 6 5 4 3 2 1

INTRODUCTION

long Life. Honey in the heart.
no evil. Thirteen thank you's.

– Guatemalan Native Blessing

Sweet. Healing. Medicinal. A little honey can make the bitterest intake seem bearable, if not pleasant. Honey is an essential ingredient in so many delicious recipes, both savory and sweet. It is also the essential element in many curative salves. Honey is a sweetness, occurring as the result of creatures doing what comes from acting according to their nature. Bees, those creatures with a reputation for working so busily, simply do what comes naturally, and produce something that is miraculous.

Making room in our hearts for the honey is a worthy endeavor, a pursuit with immediate and long term benefits. Just like the commodity of honey, the attitude of honey in the heart is delicious to all who encounter it, beginning with you.

My heart has to have room for the sweetness. There must be space made for the nectar. My days are fully occupied. The many commitments and tasks in each day would happily fill my minutes from dawn to dusk — if I let them. I get to set aside time for the sweetest things in life. I make room in my heart for "honey," those things which are sweet, healing, and restorative. At the end of the day, these small sweetnesses make up the taste that lingers. These become the real treasures that bring richness to life.

Ways to See

I explore some practical actions that create space in my heart and life for the more gracious activities, the small celebrations. I am confident you will add methods of your own as you consider all the ways you already enjoy delights in your days. Some of the most treasured joys slip through the window because we are too busy to notice. Making room in your heart hinges on noticing what is there already.

Savor

Here you will find many *invitations to celebrate* and savor the sweetness, that festive firework of a "YAY!" that explodes in your soul when something seems a bit like a holiday. I am often asked how I sustain such a cheerful outlook, in spite of the circumstances of my life being challenging. My immediate answer is that I am able to see all the "honey" in my daily life that brings me sweetness and connects me to my joy. Here I share phrases, poems and thoughts that might inspire you to see the honey in your day that you've yet to notice.

In the *Simple, good Things* section I have an eye toward the practical, with an *accounting* of actual things that drew an audible "yay" in my experience. I want my list to be the inspiration for you to begin your own list. Once you start noticing, the sweet things become a LOT easier to spot. I think of Claudia, a writing client, who was certain that her life was absent joy. In four weeks, she discovered how often she was giving one of those little "jumps for joy" in her spirit (I call them YAY) that she realized her life was actually sweeter than she imagined. The simple things managed to pass without notice in the light of all she felt compelled to accomplish in a day. Noticing one turned into two. And noticing two, she found four. Then eight.

She was excited to share with me that she was amazed at what a sweet life she has. Aptly, she observed that being aware of what is already there makes room for more!

May this book be a companion to you on a journey of discovery, a reference book, of sorts. May you have the pleasure to see and treasure the sweet celebrations that are everywhere present in your life – if you make the time and the way to see them!

Ways to See

Ways to see and savor the simple, good things in your life involves at least these six things:

 Make sure that self-care and positive choices are first on your priority list.

 Willingly set down the pain of your history and travel forward, not defining yourself with it or limiting yourself by it.

 Observe the words that fill your days and choose compliment over complaint. Be willing to discuss what went RIGHT.

 Daily visit the truth that, while you may not play all the instruments, you do conduct your own orchestra. Own your life. Live as a victor, not a victim.

 Be prepared to celebrate at all times. Live in and create an environment around you that is ready and open to guests, guests of all sort.

 Be flexible. Invite possibilities to your party. This means let go of the absolute specifics of how you think it should be and embrace the unexpected, the messy, the surprising, the startling and the extraordinary as welcome guests at your festivity, which is your life.

INVITE SELF-CARE

Having room for honey in the heart, or, being able to find the YAY in your every day, requires that you be well. Or as well as you can be. Exhaustion and dis-ease are not the finest friends of celebration and joy. Taking care, good care, of yourself is the first step toward making room in your heart for the sweetness of life. It is a kind irony that excellent self-care makes us all better able to care more deeply for others.

INVITE PAIN TO REMAIN BEHIND
AS YOU TRAVEL ON

I reinvented a holiday tradition this year. Rather than the traditional two-day cookie baking fest held in the company of two dear friends, I proposed we have a sewing fest instead. Most cookies do not appear on my menu of healthy options. I observed that cookies are quickly consumed and all the recipient is left with is an empty cookie tin. Something functional and artful would have a longer life in the experience of our giftees! My fellow elves agreed and the plan was set.

As my friend and I prepared to sew, without realizing it, we started narrating to each other all the impediments in our life to successful sewing. I regaled her with the tale of my first and last sewing project, sewn backwards in the shadow of my mother's extraordinary sewing competencies. She chronicled the various discouragements offered her by her mother. Pain had arrived, without so much as a ring at the door. Her husband, listening patiently to the tales, asked if he should phone a psychiatrist for us before we started our project. We laughed, and then marveled aloud how we had invited these stories along into our lives and allowed that pain to define our experiences. Instantly we agreed to intentionally set those stories to rest.

That holiday season was filled with the competency and joy of creating warm, fitted fingerless gloves which I gave to friends, veterans, homeless shelters and professional partners. The gloves were my invitation to make room in my heart for honey instead of harm. I packed up and moved somewhere new and left that pain behind. It was no longer useful and did not reflect the sweetness of my current experience.

I used a poetic expression to reflect on this life changing experience of intentionally replacing my story of pain with one of shared creativity and friendship. I "accidentally" held on to this story of pain… and it began to quietly impact my view of an otherwise delightful event.

> My pain stays in my wardrobe.
> To wear it is always a choice…
> The painful lyrics line my shelves.
> Each page gives pain its voice…
>
> My pain is in my history,
> Giving impulse to my present view
> It's brought me where I'm standing and now
> I'll tell a bit to you –
>
> For in the telling of the tale, pain feeds its weary soul.
> In the space it takes in telling are my hours and
> minutes – stole
>
> From the freshness of this moment, from the truth of
> this day's dawn, pain steals and rakes and rolls upon the
> soiled beauty I garden on.
>
> My pain's been ever with me.
> But I tell you this time, clear,
> It may have come this far with me,
> but today – I'll leave it here.

INVITE COMPLIMENT INSTEAD OF COMPLAINT

Like pain, complaints often slip in the door almost unnoticed. The first benefit to improving your observational skills is noticing when you've let complaint into your festivity. Complaints are sneaky. Complaining likes to masquerade as something that exerts control or authority over a situation. Ha! That is an illusion, for sure. Complaining draws attention away from all the good things that unfold. It's as if complaint puts a mask over our sight: too busy identifying what is wrong, all the things that are right march on by. While there are so many motivations behind complaining, connecting to your own reason for complaining is key to making room for honey in the heart.

Inviting compliment can be as simple as focusing on what went right with a circumstance, rather than what went wrong. Circumstances less than ideal provide their own schooling: next time, do it a different way. Imagine the pleasure of becoming passionate as you express everything that went right at work, in your commute, as you paused for a treat or enjoyed a conversation with a friend.

An old friend was in a period of overwhelm. Because she lives in a different state I wasn't connected to her challenge, I only knew that she'd been terse on occasion and hadn't answered email in a few weeks. I practiced what I believe about focusing on what is right in a circumstance. Instead of complaining to her that I felt – overlooked – I built a "Ten Things I Like About You" list and by the end of the compilation I'd remembered how busy her days are and moved away from complaint, with ease.

This is the list I sent to her:

Ten Things I Like about you

1. Your sight is clear.

2. Your ear is tuned and true.

3. You only laugh when it's funny.

4. You make cynicism soft.

5. You are profoundly empathetic.

6. You are willing to suspend supported belief for the sake of the magical possible.

7. You say, "C'mon, we're all grown ups here," and you really mean it.

8. You don't withhold goodness.

9. You want to make a difference.

10. You do make a difference.

I was certainly surprised to receive back my friend's version for me.

Ten Things my Friend Likes about me

1. Your vision is honed.

2. You take the time that's needed to speak.

3. You take the time that's needed to write.

4. You take the time to listen and make sure the listenee knows you're listening.

5. You are generous with your time and energy and …

6. You perform more small and large acts of kindness than anyone else I know.

7. You clarify in the present moment in a way that minimizes misunderstandings.

8. You laugh at my jokes.

9. You understand what I'm going to say even before I do.

10. Your work is a prayer that affects the lives of many.

What an antidote for complaining. Or general malaise. I noticed I was complaining. I changed my attitude and received an unantici-pated response. What a great turn-around! Rather than focusing on what I perceive was not going as I would like, I noticed and honored all that was going well. The results were very positive. It's one of the most treasured pieces of communication I have. I keep both messages in my mailbox and read them on days when I want to be encouraged. It demonstrates the strength of tending to compliment over complaint.

When I am inclined to complain, I ask myself to first consider my alternatives. I wonder to myself why I feel the impulse to complain and what I might actually accomplish by complaining. Lodging or voicing complaint is sometimes a viable action. Sometimes. More frequently it's like a raised hand of somebody sitting in my internal front row that wants the attention of the whole class. I call on that front row student within myself, and have a chat, before voicing the complaint externally.

I make sure I give myself a little YAY when I create an alternative action to simply complaining.

OWN YOUR LIFE

You are not invisible.

You are visible. You are your compassionate purpose, made visible in the world. You are not an invisible one among many. You have a unity with all of creation and you are a significant individual.

You are not responsible for anyone else's eyes. You are not responsible for how others see you. You are only responsible for how you see yourself. And THAT you see yourself. You must become utterly visible to you.

You cannot do everything today. You can do one thing toward everything. And you can do it today.

You cannot become perfect, because you are perfect, just as you are. Your responsibility is to be an explorer, not a tourist in this adventure that is your life and fully observe that perfection visible in the world.

Today. Right now. Embrace the questions. Fully present in this moment. Embrace the questions with integrity, laughter, and joy. Deal with the demands and the unexpected events, and live your way into the answers that are resonant for you. Both the questions and the answers only have to make sense to you. When they make sense to you it will not matter if they make sense to anyone else. In the moment you come to your own viable understanding – your heart will swing open wide for all the sweetness of your days to begin to pour in.

We embrace the elements of our days as old friends, arriving to surprise us with fresh perspective and evanescent gifts. We acknowledge even the most difficult of tasks as our teachers and endeavor to learn well, that the challenge may not need to visit us again. We sing our gratitude for the warm days and the moments when our breath comes still, deep and easy.

Own your life...
Not because you can, but because you must
Not because you think, but because you know.

Not because its easy, but because it isn't.

Not because you feel, but because you believe.

Not because its known, but because it isn't.

Not because others expect it,
        but because you demand it.

This is how art, excellence, compassion & service
live in the fully occupied moments of each day.

BE FLEXIBLE

When I was learning to drive, I proudly narrated to my dad the right way to do things. We'd be driving around town, and I'd point out an obvious driving infraction and declare, directly from the manual, all the actions that were incorrect. "Now, see, that driver went out of turn. That other guy should have let him go …"

My dad would often say, "You can be right or you can be alive." The rich meaning of that assessment continues to impact me. Being "right" isn't always the premier objective. Or even the most desirable objective. Flexibility introduces unforeseen outcomes.

Things don't always roll out "by the book." Being flexible can mean leading a parade and not knowing where you're going. Or being the last person in a parade – and knowing where you're going. Theodore Roethke inspires me each time I recite his words, "I learn by going where I have to go." Being flexible can mean being willing to participate in the party even though you're not in charge. More importantly, being flexible recognizes that you are not in charge – even when you think you are.

Flexibility is what gives loft to your view – raises you up over the fence so you can see how much fun they are having on the other side. Flexibility is the invitation for possibilities to come play in your day.

PAINTED CUP

CALIFORNIA
POPPY

FUCHSIA

PASQUEFLOWER

BLACK-EYED
SUSAN

Savor

Distilling the lessons of a sweet day into a few words is a way for me to really savor what I have learned and incorporate the truth of it into my experience. Use these condensed observations as doors through which you may walk and discover a shining gem of your own experience, knowledge and wisdom waiting for you. Also, calling to mind a set of words that are especially meaningful to you can help you as you learn to savor the best and sweetness parts of your daily life.

What to do with the important, sweetest words of your soul? Savor them – let their flavor linger. Deposit them in the bank account of your heart, paint them on your thoughts, write them on your hand, wear them like jewelry, let them lead what you teach and say, let them be the spice in your conversation, may they be the road you walk, the light of dawn that greets you and the lullaby that sends you to sleep.

In the freshness
of the dawn
we see
the truth

everything
is possible.

One must give up a little bit of road in order for poetry to pass by.

Joys move at the speed of acceptance.

When one of us lifts our vision…
it raises the possibilities for us all.

Slow long enough to marvel at the rarity
of a single leaf falling:

      swaying this way,

      and that,

      to an unheard waltz.

Wrap all your highest intentions in the ribbons of your finest
wishes and toss them into the wind for speedy delivery.

After the laundry, the epiphany.

After the sweeping, the joy.

After the predictable knocks,
the relentless press of serendipity.

Turn down the volume of demands and listen to the grace of the small, the silence, the whisper.

Watch carefully.

The most important things often appear

last on the "list."

Your festivities are the paint on the palette of your days.

Build your world
one good,
grateful word
at a time.

home *noun* 1. The place in which one lives.
2. A family in its dwelling place; household.
3. The place in which one was born, grew up,
or has lived for a long time. 4. A na...

It is perhaps incorrect to say, "I made a poem." It may be more true that a poem makes me.

Pause long enough in the unseen world to plant a seed.

If you have complaints about where you are going, change the words you're walking on.

Wow. How often do you see that? While I wasn't looking "someday" showed up.

Practice sorting through the MUCH to get to your MUST.

Everybody seemed to be having
a challenging day
until Kathleen showed up
with cupcakes.

a little cupcake
goes a long way.

I was trying to write sanity and I accidentally wrote sanctity. After thinking about it I decided they were close enough.

The ability to celebrate is a fine measure
of our capacity as a human being.

Don't limit yourself with studied successes.
Failure is underrated.
Failure's where some of the best perspectives come from.

In the greater perspective, there is no hurry.
You are always on time.

Perseverance is
the name of the path
that leads from uncertainty
to celebration.

Set aside the penchant for overwhelm and just practice.
Practice, "ONE THING at a time,"
with diligence and commitment.

The world is filled with mystery, unknown capacities,
and information that is not fully revealed. Notice. Listen.

Underneath all the noise sings a perfect and invincible soul.

What footprints will you leave in the soil of this day?

With fresh eyes we see that which has waited so patiently for notice.

Digression is an excellent research tool.

Keys from the past show up at uncanny moments
to unlock a present moment door.

Don't try to fire your inner critic –
send her to Human Resources and get her reassigned.

A writer understands there are always other words
and other ways. So it is in all things – after a certain
amount of preparation for a journey you just have
to get on the bus.

Inspiration is knowing
what time of day
and in what part of the world
to stand under a dark sky,
with an open bag,
to catch all
the stars that fall.

You can see the way to begin. Begin. Simply Begin.

We define our life each moment of the day
by what we choose to care about.

What a difference an E makes: Got to/ gEt to.

"I've GOT to get on the ferry and go to the mainland today
implies obligation."

"I GET to get on the ferry and go to the mainland today
smacks of opportunity.

"What are you doing for the holidays?"
"Having friends," she replied.
I thought that's the best gift of all – just having friends.

The accountant instructed that I must speculate on future
value and inside I knew I must politely, silently disagree.
The only value that is ever truly held is the value in this now.

Counting all competencies can be a barrier to inventive
outcomes. "I know how this should go" inevitably closes
the door on unimagined results.

I didn't know
I couldn't,
so I did.

home *noun* **1.** The place in which one live[s].
2. A family in its dwelling place; household.
3. The place in which one was born, grew up,
or has lived for a long time. **4.** A na[tural]

It's a roof until it isn't.
It's a circle until it's a dot.
It's a line until it's a border.
You're at home until you're not.
Every experience is an ending.
And it's a beginning, just as true.
The world's as big as you are,

The decision's
always up to you.

Throw open the doors of your heart wide and accept the blessings the world will offer.

The spaces between imagination and common sense are both entertaining and engaging

Generosity orchestrates the party and satisfaction finishes the event. Right actions confirm the road and Spirit affirms what you know.

Compassionate service is your colorful answer to life. Other people hear it as an unreserved, "Yes!"

Live then or now.
It's impossible to be
in two places at once.

Random just means You weren't expecting it.
Serendipity has her own plan.

All the Undone Things press their noses against the glass of
her day and breathe heavily. She closes the shade. At the
last minute she talks herself into being thankful.

Know your own answer to the "why" and let that be enough.

When you know where you're going, with conviction,
EVERY road will ultimately take you there.

It was within my scope to do a good, so I did it. That is the path to peace, isn't it?

Be good to yourself: it's the way to teach others how to treat you.

If one chooses to stand against something, the balance exists in that they also choose to stand for something.

In that split second when there's opportunity for unkindness or a sharp retort: remain silent. The whisper of pause informs a better decision.

There's music and opportunity everywhere when you're willing to see things as either miracles or magic.

Be happy. it's the taste that lingers longest on your tongue.

Simple, good Things

At a time there were structures of my life that were particularly challenging. I was losing sight of my joy and I wanted to reinforce all the graces in my ordinary days.

For a period of six months every time I was aware of something drawing a literal YAY out of me, I wrote down what prompted it. Being schooled in what a simple, good thing actually IS makes it easier to invite it on purpose. I chose this period of time, six months, for several reasons. Prevailing wisdom says that doing something for thirty days makes it a habit. I wanted my capacity to seize the simple, good things of my life to be stellar! So I committed to six months of "seeing." I knew the joys were there but I'd opted out of readily seeing them. I carried a small journal with me everywhere I went. When I was aware of that little lilt, that recognition of a sweet joy, I wrote down whatever it was that caused it.

You will discover, as I did, the things that draw out the YAY are very ordinary things. In this same period of time large events occurred, important announcements were made, significant business relationships were forged. Those are not the things found in this list. This list is made up of the things that perennially pour honey into my heart. Perhaps you will recognize some of them from your own experience. What would YOUR list look like if you kept a "YAY in ordinary days," list? What do your simple good things look like?

We tell the tale of our lives by the stories we repeat in our day.

Take that principle outward, the environments in which we work, live, and play tell stories to us and about us every day.

Coming into my space for the first time, someone would be tempted to observe the obvious: the first thing that I see when I wake up in the morning is a messy pile of books and magazines. What I see, really, is a stack of reasons to celebrate. Each thing is an invitation to celebrate and allows me to call to mind a very specific YAY which is invigorating and empowering.

In this small space I daily re-discover the stories of thoughtful friends, meaningful gestures and commitments that I have made at my core. This is just the first YAY I encounter in my day.

The opportunity to contemplate such things is a key to being able to identify the small celebrations that come to me. On those days that my eyes do not "see," and I jump into the day, pressured by that cacophony of "so much to do," I am less inclined to see the opportunity for joy, for the exclamation of pleasure and delight. Setting the tone at the start of my day is significant, if not essential.

What is the first thing you set your sights upon in the morning? And how do you invite yourself in to a day that you intend to savor? I've shared with you a window into my way, now take a good look at your way.

It was invigorating and illuminating to write down the things that made me jump up for joy inside. I am not going to share every single thing I wrote, because there are just too many. I've eliminated the things that I repeated and some things that just wouldn't make sense to anyone but me.
Otherwise, this is the list as it evolved over six months. I hope it inspires you to savor and start your own list!

MY EVERY DAY LIST OF YAY'S

The List — Seeing and Savoring the Simple Good Things Every Day (The YAY in EverYdAY)

Do not give regret berth in my decisions.

Find heart shaped rocks while walking the beach.

Find money in the pocket of an old coat.

Get a "just because" card in the mail from a friend.
(an actual card with a postage stamp on it!). Thank the
postal carrier for consistent service.

Begin at O Dark Thirty, enthusiastic and fully awake.

Discover an old letter from a childhood friend.

Pick up a bright, shiny penny while on a walk.

Open eyes to see the precious
in an ordinary exchange.

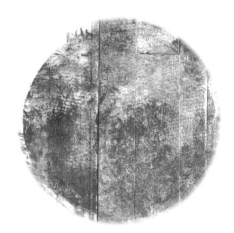

Use a brand new toothbrush.

The dog finally obeys a "sit stay" command.

Count all the can's in my diet, not the "can'ts."

Watch a friend enjoy every bite of their favorite pie
while I savor a fresh cup of coffee.

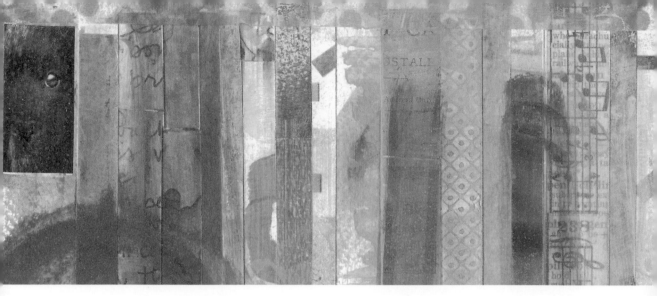

Laugh at ducks waddling comically in an uneven line.

Use sparkle fixative instead of ordinary glue.

Recognize a patch of local land conserved as a wilderness legacy.

Be surprised by an out of the blue phone call from an old friend.

Hold hands while walking to the store with the love of my life.

Post a beautiful picture on Facebook with a positive statement and get tons of great comments.

Have exact change.

make all the green lights and arrive early.

Sing in the car and remember all the words.

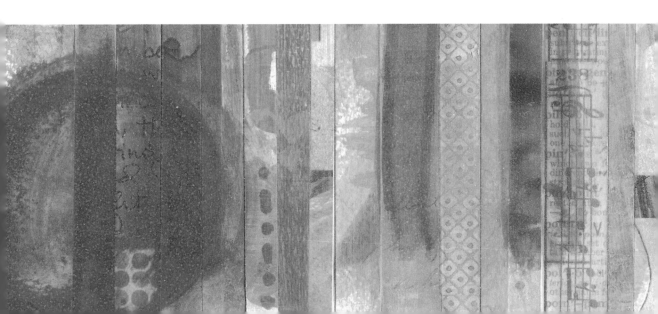

Move from Do to DONE and check everything off my list. "Complete" sounds so much better than "almost done."

Get a great idea, capture it in writing and take several actions toward it. Get another great idea and give it to someone who might begin to implement it.

Send a card for no particular reason... Make something simple and beautiful, wrap it up and send it to a far away friend for no particular reason other than I'm thinking of her.

Doodling.

Watch a mom and a daughter giggle together.

Make and eat a caramel apple.

Scratch the ears of a dog that was already happy.

See the smile when I call my husband "John Wayne."

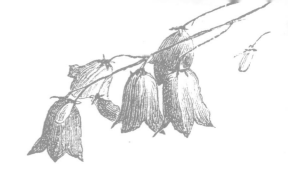

Watch my dog make a nest out of a blanket.

Be awakened by the tap of a gentle paw.

Enjoy coffee served in bed.

Make nutritional choices that support my well being.

Receive sincere praise from an absolute stranger.

Climb into smooth, clean sheets.

Think about the "What are your fifteen favorite books?" question.

Know an entire "day off" stretches out before me.

Be grateful for all the "enough" in my life.

Talk about all the ways I had fun yesterday.

Discuss everything that went right.

Wear flannel pajamas on a cold morning.

Think of the friend
who made the
quilt

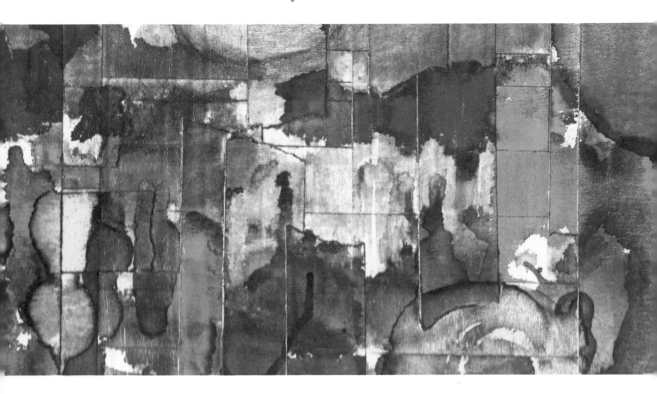

at the foot of my bed.

Shop for Christmas gift MAKING supplies.

Watch a kid's film and love the goodness in it.

Know and keep a secret honorably.

Plan a close-to-home holiday.

gratitude

gratitude

gratitude

Clean the house as a team.

Put my favorite French linen on the table.

Aware that my life is a walking poem, meditation, praise and prayer.

Anticipate the start of my work week.

· · · · · · · · · · · · · · · · · ·

Adopt an active military service person and send packages and cards.

Kind words spoken easily.

A best friend who remembers me and reflects on our shared good times.

Laugh that our dog is so long that she has two zip codes.

Delighted that my husband's malady leaves him pain free for long stretches of days.

Get a state of the art piece of equipment.

The synchronicity of calling a friend who says, "I was just coming to the phone to call you."

Choose flexibility over impatience.

Understand dog talk.

See three black Labrador retrievers in one afternoon.

Honor my friend's six months of sobriety.

Learn what adjustments to a bread recipe won't work and watch the birds benefit from my lesson.

Choose compassion over conflict and have a conversation instead of a fight.

Recognize a kindred spirit in a new friendship.

Take a personal stand on the issue of bullying.

Have an unlimited number of gold stars to distribute.

Spot a bald eagle resting atop a sailboat mast.

Love the breathless view of a giant mirror-like harbor.

Incorporate a little yoga into my everyday routine.

Savor the end of a fabulous book.

Love myself including my shortcomings.

Warrior love – speak the truth and move on.

Certainty, safety and success to those who serve and protect.

Ability to give a little in the face of a need that is large.

Love 'em - just as they are -
not as I think they should be or
could be.

Water the "wishing tree" that grows in the soil of my own soul.

Tell the truth with sensitive grace.

Be grateful that Thomas Jefferson changed "Pursuit of Property," to "Pursuit of Happiness."

Pay the difference on a stranger's "postage due."

Criticism provides an open door to my unseen possibilities.

Waking to the cacophony of bird chatter outside the window.

An excellent title for a book occurs to me and I wonder if
I'll be the one to write it.

Forgive a debt.

Help a friend in a practical and immediate way.

Follow a whim to an amazing conclusion.

Make up a song inadvertently.

Enjoy that it's Friday.

Make it through a meltdown
with no collateral damage.

Circumstances do not determine my state of being.

Remember that Camus said, "The meaning of life is to live a meaningful life."

Be a tourist in my own backyard.

The holy opportunity in each day to do work I love.

The privilege of casting my vote.

The freedom to banish the bitterness roaming the halls of my soul.

Establish new patterns instead of succumbing to habit.

open to discovery and laugh that
it can look like failure.

Accept a compliment with grace and ease.

Watch long held dreams unfold.

Recognize strength that occasionally masquerades as
weakness.

Love and admire my country in spite of challenge
and crisis.

BE a good friend along with HAVE a good friend.

Realize that I didn't complain once
about anything all day long.

afterword

This Is What you Shall Do...

Live closer, every moment of your life, to that thing that quickens your spirit and makes you sing; give when you can and help as you must; listen longer and speak less, speak more when the words are of healing and love and appreciation; recognize that when you contribute good anywhere you change the world; forgive more and judge less; accept more and criticize less; be certain of what you know while knowing you know practically nothing; embrace today's bad news as tomorrow's breakthrough and know you will live through it and you will thrive; contribute to your own health and set aside apology and justification; ring the bell at the top of your own hill, squeeze the precious goodness out of the fruit of your own harvest and pour your own cup full, first, and then offer to fill the cups of others.

In this, and in all the ways you imagine, you will always be able to see and savor the simple good things, the sweet honey of life.

To Our Readers

Conari Press, an imprint of Red Wheel/Weiser, publishes books on topics ranging from spirituality, personal growth, and relationships to women's issues, parenting, and social issues. Our mission is to publish quality books that will make a difference in people's lives—how we feel about ourselves and how we relate to one another. We value integrity, compassion, and receptivity, both in the books we publish and in the way we do business.

Our readers are our most important resource, and we appreciate your input, suggestions, and ideas about what you would like to see published.

Visit our website *www.redwheelweiser.com* where you can learn about our upcoming books and free downloads, and be sure to go to *www.redwheelweiser.com/newsletter/* to sign up for newsletters and exclusive offers.

You can also contact us at info@redwheelweiser.com.

Conari Press
an imprint of Red Wheel/Weiser, llc
665 Third Street, Suite 400
San Francisco, CA 94107